CW01095356

The Forgetting and Remembering of Air

Sue Hubbard is an award-winning poet, novelist and freelance art critic. Twice winner of the London Writers competition and a Hawthornden Fellow, she has published two collections of poetry *Everything Begins with the Skin*, (Enitharmon) and *Ghost Station*, (Salt) and a limited edition of poems, illustrated by Donald Teskey, *The Idea of Islands* (Occasional Press, Ireland). Her first novel, *Depth of Field*, was published by Dewi Lewis and her acclaimed short story collection, *Rothko's Red*, by Salt. The Poetry Society's only official Public Art poet, she was responsible for London's largest public art poem at Waterloo. Awarded two prestigious residences to Yaddo, USA, she was also the recipient of a major Arts Council Literary Award for her novel, *Girl in White*, published by Cinnamon Press. Her poems have been broadcast on Radio 3 and 4.

As an art critic she has contributed regularly to *Time Out*, the *New Statesman* and *The Independent*, and to a range of art magazines, including *Apollo*, *Tate* and the *RA* magazine. Her collected art writings, *Adventures in Art*, were published by Other Criteria in 2011.

In this, her third collection, she meditates both on art and the natural world. By going to the extreme edge of western Ireland, to a Cornish beach, to the rim of the Solway Firth and the mouth of the Thames she explores, in these disarmingly direct poems in a language that is both muscular and painterly, the illusion of romantic love and the letting go of childhood grief. In the central section, based on paintings by the artist Rachel Howard, she examines the psychology of different women in extremis.

The Forgetting and Remembering of Air

by

SUE HUBBARD

For Sarah
with good wishes,
Sue
2015

SALT

CROMER

PUBLISHED BY SALT PUBLISHING
12 Norwich Road, Cromer, Norfolk NR27 0AX

© Sue Hubbard, 2013

Salt Publishing 2013

Printed in Great Britain by the MPG Books Group, Bodmin and King's Lynn

Typeset in Paperback 9 / 13

ISBN 978 1 907773 39 6 hardback

1 3 5 7 9 8 6 4 2

Contents

Acknowledgements

Hens was published in the online magazine *Ink, Sweat and Tears,* The Policeman's Daughter was first published in *Art World Magazine* and appeared in the Seren Anthology: *Tokens for the Foundlings.* Naked Portrait was commissioned by the Tate for their online poetry series. Edge was written during a residency at the De La Warr Pavilion during ArchiTEXT week 2003. Versions of Smokers, Nits, Figs and Klein's Blue were published in the *Bow-Wow Shop.* After Degas was first published in *Oxford Poets 2000* (Carcanet). Symmetry was shortlisted in the Cardiff Poetry Competition. Migrations and Mist appeared in *A Room to Live In: A Kettle's Yard Anthology* (Salt) and all the poems in the section The Idea of Islands, except Uíbh Ráthach and Dreaming of Islands, were first published in a limited edition under that title by Occasional Press, Ireland, with drawings by Donald Teskey in 2010. Ballinskelligs and The Ice Ship were published in *The Irish Times.*

Particular thanks are due to Linda Rose Parkes and Michael Freeman for their hospitality whilst editing these poems and to Linda's insightful criticism, also to Martyn Crucefix and Stephen Duncan for their helpful contributions and to the Cill Rialaig project and Hawthornden for the space to write many of these poems.

For the writer, discovering the work he will write is both like a miracle and a wound, like the miracle of the wound.

The Book of Questions: EDMOND JABÈS

I

A Meaningful Speech

A Meaningful Speech

What do things know?
The asphalt road with its marching pylons
and telephone wires reverberating
with a thousand hidden voices,
or those giant turbines embedded
in the waves of the Solway Firth,
their long white necks holding up the membrane of sky
as the tide rushes in like an invading army.
Or this biro, or sheet of cheap lined paper,
the empty milk carton and kettle beside the sink?
Do they, deep in their rigid forms,
still carry a memory of earth, the vibrations
and rhythms of rock, of metal and clay?
Walking through the wooded glen I listen
to the silence of trees, taste
the fungal fragrance of air as each thing watches.
And then the rain, drenching the mulch
of dead leaves, soaking the muddy path.
Nobody started it, no one will stop it.
It will take as long as it wants this rain,
drenching me and the homely brown cow
with the film-star fringe over in the far field
with her suckling calf; the oaks, the bracken,
the stones, and for as long as it speaks, I'll listen.

The Forgetting and Remembering of Air

Early morning, and beyond this small window
a whiteness spreads, descending
to water as the thin light of the Solway Firth
draws down the sky to merge
in a vanishing point with the grey strait
along the Workington shore,
as the tide empties its lungs
across the wide sands.
How often we speak of the imperceptible gaps
between people and trees and clouds
as empty space, take for granted the air,
that continual flow, in and out, feathering
the nostrils so there seems no connection
between inner and outer, the world and skin,
as we forget what is invisible, the richness
of the present and now.
But we are the air; and trees speak
with the same breath, jostled by wind,
each fragile leaf with its own distinctive voice.
Listen to the murmurs of river on stone,
the whispers of that abandoned house
on the tip of the headland where
an empty staircase reaches up to
cobwebbed rooms once filled with living breath.
What do they tell us?
That we are one great lung, breathing
the world into and out of itself: the thrift,
the foxglove and bracken fringing the sandy

footpath to the beach, the rainclouds banking
across the glen, as we quietly inhale
the damp opacity of sea and sky and wind.

High Winds

All morning I walk through the wood
in search of a poem as the wind
sweeps through the tall beeches

in a rushing tide; each branch
each word unstable
and I am all at sea

as if high in the swaying crows' nest
of some sailing ship
mid-Atlantic,

buffeted by a churning swell,
while willow-pattern teacups
slide across tables

and the young girl in an *eau-de-Nil* dress
nervously lifts a stray strand of hair,
as the waves surge in

engulfing sheet music,
a powder puff,
a single satin shoe.

Only the living take things for granted,
until that icy tide closes over us
and all the old words drown.

The Ice Ship

All night it is day. Glycerine shadows fuse sea and
    sky into something indivisible. Hoar-frost and snow mingle with hail.
This is the end of the inhabitable world we are so far north.

Snow-clad mountains spit fire, icebergs drift
    in a boiling swell, piercing the pale sun in its net of frosty air.
We have been at sea for days.

Ice-cold, iron-cold, our lungs tense against the razor chill,
    it could be the moon we are so distant from ourselves.
Dreaming and loving here are the same hunger

as we wander in watery exile, storm-beaten
    by perishing winds. Ahead the glacial hull looms
spectral in the crushing heaves of pack-ice,

 trapped like a fisherman's float
    in the mouth of a silver carp. Tattered sails,
fragments of mast, poke from their crystal coffin

like splintered whale-bone, trepanning the empty heart of blue.
    For thirteen years they have waited, penitent
as glass angels, black lips welded to alabaster tongues,

untold tales frost-bitten in their throats. Alone
    at his log, the Captain holds patient vigil,
awaiting a huff of divine breath.

So far from home, we glide directionless
    beneath the bald sun
through cerulean ice-fields, past glacial slabs

too cold even for sea birds,
    as grievous and exhausted
we give ourselves up to what we've become.

riverrun

bird song and in the wet woods
shattered trees brittle as promises
below in the dark ravine
the brown Esk
whirlsover
back and round
protruding stones
poking like bones
through the March swell
bubbles breaking
into rills of scummy water
every surge is different
like the experience
of love as the stream
thrusts on inscrutable
indifferent to be caught
in a knot of twigs
a blue plastic bag
only to escape quick as Houdini
beneath a smashed log the burn chokes
flecks of spittle
churn up the slop
of winter leaves
gaseous and fermenting
in the viscous mud
before rushing on again
as if to arrive nowhere in particular
will somehow be different
standing in this
thin wind between

Valentine's and Easter
        I hold my breath
            and listen to the wood
            waiting for something to happen
as a small brown bird darts out
on the path ahead –
but that is all

Tip

There are no trees, only horizons and the quiet exhalation of tides
seeping across the silted marshes like primal breath cleansing

the malarial plagues and fevers that once stalked these sodden lands.
Between dreams of wilderness and the city's dark stink, beyond the rim

of reeds and reclaimed pasture, vast tankers and container ships
from Medway, Sheerness and Chatham float, silent as refugees, past pylons

and refineries, their rusting hulks brown as the throat of water that pours
through the estuary's open mouth into the cleansing sea.

Beneath the sky's heavy tarpaulin, redshank and black-headed gulls gather
along the strip of foreshore where graveyards of china lie buried

in the flats; fragments of Spode, tin ware, earthen ware, cream ware,
a sliver of Sunday saucer with its faded rose, the handle of a chamber pot,

an old man's spittoon. And on the creek's small beach
a crunch of glass: medicine, milk, soda and poison bottles

in amber, blue and green, lying like jewels buried in the mud,
remnants of lives lived amid soot-filled streets,

the close-shouldered houses. I excavate the layers then, in the spitting
    rain,
carry back green bottles pitted with river-water beneath my coat.

I want to offer you one, something rescued from the fragments,
but storm clouds gather and we hurry for the car

as a murmur of starlings wheels above the wetlands,
scribbling across the slate sky that which we cannot say.

Klein's Blue

Of the three boys
on a beach
who divided up the world

he got the sky
and signed his name
on its pristine surface,

then lay back to look up
at what he had created
thinking that God

must be envious.
But how he hated the birds
that flew across his perfect,

cloudless canvas
boring holes into his
most beautiful work.

Searching for a blue to beat
the creator at his own game
he suspended pure pigment,

particles of heaven,
in crystal resin. Young girls,
their breasts and pubic hair

smeared in ultramarine
pinned down his sky
as he orchestrated them

in tuxedo and white gloves;
though the lines
of the actual body

held no interest,
for at night he dreamt only
of alchemy, of gravity and grace,

of stepping from that high
window to float above the city street
in a void of endless blue.

White Canvas

Porthmeor beach, St. Ives.

Such blue that only a painter's
pigment can achieve a simile.
I try to write a line of colour,

but words are a string of biro scrawls
without air or light or hue,
reflecting neither the translucency

of sea or sky, nor the flat spare
canvas of creamy sand washed
by the sucking tide

that rims the far patch of ultramarine
where black-suited surfers bob
like seals between red and yellow flags.

Or further out, that band of cobalt –
darkened by hidden rocks –
where signatures of surf scrawl

against the curved horizon
and the ocean meets
a water-colour haze.

Across wet sands
Magritte clouds caste
shadows, black as dogs, between

striped windbreaks rowed
like modernist paintings
   in blue and white and green.

If words were colours,
I would paint the welkin
   hyacinth, azure, Prussian blue,

as summer slips away
and gulls tilt their wings
   against the sail-white page.

After Degas

Her young body lies a twisted *S*
in the pool of her black skirt,
the encased striations of her pin-

striped blouse, on a cool mattress
of sand under the tilted parasol.
Beneath closed eye-lids

she breathes the thick
smell of surf and shore, hears
the yelp of damp dogs, the distant

shrieks of children running barefoot beneath the pewter sky,
as her sodden hair pours

onto the spread white cloth
where her mother drags and
and drags the shark-toothed comb

through the tangled mass.
She flinches, surfacing from day-
dreams: fat-bellied sails of distant

ships taut as bare skin, fish-tang
of rigging, the heave and heft
of dripping nets, wind unhooking her

like the steel eyelets on her bodice,
a taste of salt on her lips.

Nits

You always leave the sink
stippled with black stubble;
a tidemark of drying foam
beached on white porcelain.
Yet even as I *Jiff* it clean
sluice the bowl of debris,
polish plug and taps,
we are back in that cold bathroom,
your small body shivering
inside your Ladybird airtex vest,
towel draped prize-fighter-style
around your shoulders,
as acrid fumes smart our eyes,
gag in our throats and you try
to shove me off, resist
the vicious comb
as it ploughs furrows through
your noxious, tousled hair;
the sink filling with a shower
of snowy eggs and broken black bodies.
After I'd shampoo you clean
with a scent of *Pine Wood*
or *Apple Glades*,
a halo of suds
ringing your bowed head.

Love in Whitstable

For Louie

Turning up old photos I thought
I'd lost I come across you,
three year old boy, naked on a silver beach,
silhouetted against the sinking sun,

arms raised above your white-blond
head like some feral child.
In the waning light, the pewter sands
glisten as if tarnished by moonlight,

revealing the mud flats the distant tide's
left behind. Believe me, if I could, I'd
make a deal with that God I hardly believe in,
just to show you what it takes to be here.

For happiness, I want to tell you,
comes unexpected
as those iridescent shells we found
near the lugworms' coiled casts.

Open your heart like a door
and listen as the world hums quietly
to itself, to those far waves exhaling
their own tremendous music.

Blood Paintings

After Andy Goldsworthy

Once he had the skin cut clean
from the bone,
edging each furry leg with the tip

of his knife along the shaft of shin,
as if peeling off a woman's silk stocking,
he was surprised by the amount of blood.

He had hit the hare head-on
coming home over the hill
in the winter gloaming,

knew its back was broken
by the thud, then stopped
to grab it by the ears

slinging the still warm body
limp on the seat beside him,
the scent of gut and fur

mingling with the reek
of muddy leather. Later,
he stuffed the sac of its stomach

with blood and snow,
hanging it by its hind legs
from a hook in the Dutch interior

of the cold pantry
so the melting mess dripped
through its mouth and nostrils,

each droplet pooling
on the white sheet
dark as virgin's rose.

Songs of Andalucía

The heat has ended and down in the valley
the village dogs are barking,
their pink tongues flapping between
sharp teeth like slivers of Iberian ham.
Around the pleated sandstone crags
the thunder rumbles, while on the roof
the workman sends out clouds of concrete
that mingle to mud in the rain.
And I imagine how, at the end of the day,
he'll open a can of beer –
while his ample wife chops tomatoes
in their kitchen, two damp rings staining
the armpits of her blouse – as he lays
his dusty head upon her shoulder
and slips a calloused hand beneath
the satin – in a gesture that, from here,
looks something like love.

2.

The mountain reflects back its emptiness
as I stand at the window in this colossal dark.
There is no moon, no stars, nothing to feel

romantic about, only the rustle of reeds
in the dry river bed and the solitary bark
of a dog. I do not know this place,

but there must be something to be learnt
from watching the sheet lightning streak
across the sky silhouetting the wrecked building,

the radio pylon on the far ridge, the dirt track
that leads, eventually, to the sea.
Across the valley, a solitary light glimmers where

someone else climbs from a tousled bed to make tea.
The night ahead seems endless; but there's nothing
to be done, except patiently wait for dawn.

Symmetry

Your need for form takes over,
the precision of black trouser belt

straightened to the edge
of boxer shorts, white fields of paper

set square, as if such
rituals of alignment might ward off

ancient hurts buried deep
as sapphires in

some dark, dank Indian mine.
Your world is a cracked mirror

where the checking
and rechecking of closed

refrigerator doors, the back
window's bolted lock, those three

turns of the washroom tap before
the scrubbing of clean hands

might reconstruct some necessary
order, give answers

to those questions
you don't even understand

as you run from a God
you can no longer trust,

rinsing the taste of shit you fear
lingering on your lips.

I don't know what I want
from you here in this

darkened room amid
these shadows of fading

October light; just to take
your brown hand in my white

and lay our palms edge to edge
to measure the span of friendship,

its exact alignment, as Galileo once
measured the distance between sun and moon,

the earth and far-off stars,
then close your fingers in a fist

disrupting the precise symmetry –
like this, like this.

Conversation With a Bowl

Speckled as a Maran's egg, the curved glaze of your surface
meets my gaze as the morning sun pours through the kitchen window

bruising the wound of your chipped lip. Among the knife-scars on the
 deal table
you sit replete amid your history: the provider of children's porridge,
 a container

for damsons and ripe blackberries picked from the edge of an
 autumn field,
the smudges of the potter's fingertips overlaid by those of more
 recent claim.

I know you bowl; have lived with you. Yet still you hold fast your
 secrets;
for to see your far edge, hidden like the dark side of the moon, I must
 turn you

in my hand or, else, walk round the table, when, of course, it will have
 disappeared.
Yet still I feel your entirety; the way, over the years, you've hunkered
 on the shelf

observing the birth of children, the death of marriages, how you hold
 your presence
as you present one face to the evening lamp, another to the checked
 curtains and blue door.

When I peer into your reflections darkened, in the evening, by
    shadows of wet pine
outside the window, I enter new worlds. I cannot exhaust you simply
    by looking,

cannot reach the secret interior of your dense clay body, the essence
    of the patterns
trapped between your fired layers. Each time I return to your
    polished slipware

you change with my mood, shift with the inflexions of the rain-filled
    afternoon.
Like a casual lover you reveal yourself only by withholding, so I'd
    have

to break you to discover your structure, your true heart. Yet caressing
your grainy surface I feel touched: a single unity in this shifting world.

Keeping Hens

She wore yellow *Marigold* gloves
to catch them, needing fleece-lined
rubber between their feathers

and her fear – the aerated bones
hollow as straws, the flapping flightless
wings – that carried them no further

than the shed roof when she shooed them,
to perch in the eaves away
from the murderous fox.

Mornings they would scramble,
leap-frog over other feathered backs,
wobbling liver combs and beady eyes,

bobbing on string necks, like prisoners
at the wire, waiting for the steaming mash
and corn she brought in a white basin.

She hated the giblet rawness, the scraggy
throats of those hen-pecked by the flock.
He wondered why she bothered

heaving the heavy meal-sacks, collecting
kitchen scraps, could not share
in the romance of it, their own fresh eggs.

Still she persisted; squelching ankle-deep
through March mud to collect
a mottled clutch, washing the streaked

lime-white shit, the caked dirt,
from warm shells beneath the running tap
as if they were all her own work.

The Policeman's Daughter

After Paula Rego

There she sits in her white dress,
all Goody-Two-Shoes, eyes downcast,
the little Miss Prim.

But she doesn't fool me
with all that elbow grease furiously
polishing his black boots at the kitchen table.

Look how her bare arm, fat as a ham,
disappears right down to the heel.
She'd have him believe she was a real

Daddy's girl. Twists him round her little
finger. But the set of her mouth, I know that.
The I-dare-you-to-tell clench of her jaw

when she pinches me under the gingham
cloth, sticks pins through the wings
of blue bottles she catches

in a sugar jar on the ledge of our attic
window, then, as they squirm, fixes them
to her dress, two shimmering brooches.

I've seen that flicker of a smile,
curled at the corner of her lips,
spread across her mouth like a kiss.

Smokers

You hardly ever see them now, banned from every pub and bar,
   except outside on the pavement's edge, girls with bare midriffs
and mottled legs in minis, shivering in the cold, taking a drag,
   or office workers in the Square Mile, their shoulders hunched
against the chill, insisting on a lunchtime thrill of just another fag.

And pipes? Well, who remembers those? How easily it comes back
   to me, my father standing by the fire, the spills,
the blade for scraping ash, those wire pipe cleaners used to plumb
   the wooden stem that we twisted into little men,
 the way he tapped the bowl against the red brick hearth.

And I remember how I could hardly speak and hid
   my heart behind those weak stuttered syllables, as in the gloaming
of that smoke-filled gloom, I longed to become what I could never be,
   a light between despair and luminosity: his chosen girl –
and how the yearning only made the room feel darker.

Naked Portrait 1972-3

After Lucian Freud

I know this room as well as any prisoner
knows his cell, the harsh white pallor

tingeing the calamine rawness
of my skin infirmary green as pinioned

by his gaze I lie exposed across this
old brass bed, drowned cadaver on

a mortician's marble slab. Though I give
everything I have, hold nothing back,

he barely sees me. A woman, a dog
for him they're the same. At night

he breathes in my civet sweetness, by day
I'm an experiment in bald flesh;

nipples, pubic hair, my open thighs
terrain for his palette knife, the sable

brushes lying on the paint-clotted stool.
Crow-like he picks me clean.

My fan of fallen hair offers no protection
as he peels back my paper skin.

Outside his high windows
the winter morning is dark with rain;

buses, taxis, cyclists
swish through the glistening

mica streets as if there was
somewhere they needed to go.

Radio Days

Hilversum, Lille, Munich, Droitwich,
and *Moscow* . . . I travelled guided only
by my trusty Ever Ready beam

through snowstorms of sound
beneath the paisley eiderdown,
sliding Bakelite knobs between

Home and *Light* and the sovereign strains
of Lillibulero in search of *Luxembourg,*
where Horace Bachelor of Keynsham

offered foolproof schemes for scooping
pools, between Elvis's Blue Suede Shoes
and Cliff's Walkin', Talkin' Livin' Doll;

ghost stations that promised
escape from the narrow sorrows
of neat suburbia.

Though I've learnt to live
with those old griefs, memories
flutter like the needle across a dial

as flurries of snow fall outside,
swirls of white sound stuttering
in the moonless dark.

Figs

Four warm figs stuffed
  with bacon and blue cheese

sit in the middle of a square white
  plate, while you, dapper at ninety

in your Savile Row grey,
  flirt with the Polish waitress.

You still have an eye
  for a pretty girl. Then they come:

the questions as to why I'm not
  close to my sister or have a 'nice' man

and while you insist on coffee,
  I am mute, unable to speak

of the wedge you drove between
  your two daughters, the compliant

and the 'difficult', of how
  I could never be the golden girl

of your imagining. You who lacerated
  me with a tongue laced

with your own fear of failure.
  And I wonder, now, if I should

tell you how I was hardly able to live,
  yet know you could not bear

what such telling would call up in you.
  Then you climb, unsteadily,

into the taxi, take my hand in yours
  and tell me you love me;

your rheumy eyes filling
  with tears, your face crumpling

like a child's at an unanswered
  question, so I am crushed

by the weight of your regret,
  as the chill wind blows along

the Embankment, corrugating
  the ash-grey water

and I am left cradling your words
  in my freezing hands.

Meeting

I have glimpsed that moment when the sun
breaks through to illuminate the crumbling mortar

of the garden wall, that fragile glint
burnishing the straggling nasturtiums,

the pots of rosemary, sage and withered
lemon balm. It's there that I've seen her,

that other ghostly self
beyond the kitchen window:

fragile, young, breasts tender against
the weave of her cotton shirt, her head

held like a thrush's listening
as she stands barefoot among blown leaves

gathered on the gravel path.
And I can see from her lips, moist

and parted as if about to ask a question,
that the difference between us is

that she believes in a future; still dreams
of a room filled with lamplight

where an ocean of damp sheets lies
in a roll of white surf across the brass bed.

And I want to rinse this ring of suds
from my wrists and go into

that October garden,
out among the shadows of rust

and fern, to take her in my arms
and promise

she will live this life better,
that she will not be found wanting.

II

Over the Rainbow

The Fall

Monument, Charing Cross, 1838

A normal Wednesday; the streets full of the stamp
  and snort of horses, cobbles covered ankle-deep
with filth and mire and a noxious steam rising to mingle
  with the blanket of smog above the blackened chimneys,
as dogs bark and drovers steer bellowing cattle towards the Strand.

You pay your sixpence; say you're awaiting friends
  as you pass the time of day, then twenty minutes later
announce you'll make the ascent alone. But some sixth sense
  makes me look up to catch you plunging headlong through
the sky; your black silks billowing like Icarus's tattered wings.

Crumpled as a pile of used laundry, you lie amid the smashed lilac
  and fallen bird-cage, your spine snapped like a twig,
your left arm ripped off by the iron rail, yet your pretty face
  in no way disfigured save for the coagulation of blood forced
from your eyes and nostrils by the violence of the blow.

Then the shoving, yelling crowd: police, the screeching women.
  None guessing what had brought you here.
Now someone pushes through the throng to lower
  your ripped dress, cover the exposed undergarments,
as if sweeping balls of dust under the vestibule carpet.

Dora

He first deceased, she for a little tried
To live without him, liked it NOT, and died.

SIR HENRY WOTTON

Wrapped in your old purple dressing gown,
the whiff of patchouli still clinging from your beard,

my Chinese yellow hanging limp upon the door,
the geranium on the mantel reflected in the mirror

that returns my gaze: large blue eyes revealing nothing,
as a glass door betrays only a shimmer reflected

off the sea. Youthful, boyish, awkward, with pudding basin hair –
until you move in close and catch the web of lines,

the darkly bruised, almost battered sockets.
Although I longed to go, Ralph saved me from the gas;

hauling me back like a fish on a line.
Now, quiet as a jury, weeping willows gather

outside my window to witness the satin barrel
nuzzled against flushed skin. For what use is painting now?

Everything was for you. Oh darling Lytton,
you are dead and I can tell you nothing.

Eva

'When the Führer has won the war, he has promised me that I can go to
Hollywood and play my own part in the film of our life story.'

Not long out of the convent, balanced on Herr Hoffmann's ladder
in search of files, I knew, when you entered the studio you were
    looking

at my legs, that the hem of my newly shortened skirt wasn't straight.
With your funny moustache, English coat and big felt hat,

I saw my destiny – though you forbade me dance or smoke,
abandoned me to brood and pine, do gymnastics by the lake.

Afternoons I'd shop for Ferragamo shoes, change and re-change my
    dress,
read romantic novels while you built an Empire to last a thousand
    years.

Betrothed to the Nation you'd say I was your secretary when you
    dined at
The Berghof with generals and dukes, refused me marriage for fear
    your

children might be mad. It wasn't much of a wedding, though I'd
    waited
15 years: your favourite black dress and diamond watch, I had my hair

especially curled. Alone amid the long shadows of the bunker, you
    gave me
my wedding gift, the thin glass vial placed like a fresh-water pearl in
    my palm.

I understood what was expected as the radio announced the Russians
    closing
in, saw what you'd done to Blondi. Man and wife for less than 40
    hours.

Now I, too, will be etched on the glorious tomb of history,
this trace of bitter almonds smeared like your last kiss upon my lips.

Eve Arnold Remembers

Not even a blonde. That came later.
She was born brunette, Norma, a sad neglected child,
her mother in an institution for the crazed.
In the orphanage she told stories – how Cary Grant
was her father who'd carry her off, away from
the reek of poverty that seeped beneath
the chipped green doors, the echoing linoleum
scrubbed with carbolic to a God-fearing shine,
those grey-tinged sheets stale with another's breath.
But in front of my lens her skin had that special glow.
The walk, the wiggle, the pout, you know,
were all invented. I shot her in leopard-skin,
lithe among the long grass,
and poised beneath a parasol, her white
broderie anglaise cinched tight to give an hour-glass waist,
then in front of the washroom glass with it hitched,
knowingly, around her thighs.
Even towards the end, dizzy with bourbon and Nembutal
she gave everything she had, as if the camera
was her one true love. Yet when you looked deep
into her eyes she had already become a ghost.
They had to smash in the door with a poker,
found her nude body face down, sprawled
diagonally across the bed, a bottle of pills,
and her left hand touching the ivory telephone
as if there was still one last thing she wanted to say.

Over the Rainbow

June, the Chelsea streets blousy with petrol fumes
and dust, and across the cobbled mews
the private suddenly exposed like a glimpse
of dirty washing as a door bursts open
and she runs flushed, mascara-streaked,
into the evening air. He is her fifth.
Married a hundred days and nothing
but shouting. There are rumours that he's gay.
Next morning he's woken from a drunken sleep
by a trilling phone, discovers the bathroom locked,
the front door flung open. Clambering over the roof
he finds her slumped on the toilet,
dry blood caked around her mouth and nostrils.
They carry away her emaciated frame, draped
like a folded coat across the policeman's arm,
hidden by a blanket. Forty-seven and fading fast,
past the middle way. But oh, how we loved her;
forgave that broken voice, the barbiturate slur
as we watched Dorothy's ruby slippers
bear our childhood dreams to the Emerald City,
just a step beyond the rain.

Note for Ted

From Assia

She was always there between us,
the power of her words cross-stitching her name
Lilliputian across your chest,
those nimble fingers binding your bony plectrum
with strands of her Aryan hair.
I daughter of Tel Aviv, sister of Buchenwald,
a mere footnote,
lost you to your guilt and her ghost.

Though I cried out to your big hands,
the inside of your wrists, the long bones of your dear thighs,
called and called through the wound of my oesophagus –
my throat raw as the larynx of a silenced lark –
                                   you didn't hear me.

Yet when I pulled away you hunted me
down like my own private Nazi guard.
In bed you always gave off a butcher's smell;
that tang of offal, liver and lungs.

Now the night-blackened windows stare at me
ashamed as I carry our sleeping child, wrapped
in a paisley eiderdown, along the cold linoleum
to the horse-hair mattress pulled from our bed,
before the oven door –

you never loved us enough for me to leave her here.
Switching off the kitchen light, I turn on the taps
and curl beside her listening to the hum

of the fridge, the Mayflower cooker putt-putting
in the dark, our heads so close
I can smell the Vosene in her new-washed hair.

Last Supper

After Diane Arbus

Is this it? The lights of Manhattan blinking
like a succession of random thoughts,
a string of fake pearls strung across
the dark city, leading nowhere.
Nothing is easier than self-deceit. The thing
that's important is to know that you don't know.
I flip through the index of memories
to make sense of what brought me here:
a childhood of cooks and chauffeurs
in that Central Park apartment,
the public rooms filled with reproduction
Louise Quinze – everything for show –
and me home alone like a princess in some movie set
in Transylvania, my mother depressed, my father
absent at Russek's Fur Store selling sable pelts
to wealthy Jewish women.
A photograph is a secret about a secret.
Taking pictures was like tiptoeing into the kitchen
late at night to steal Oreo cookies.
I loved those freaks: the transvestites, strippers
and Jewish giant, the wealthy women with faces
like broken glass, those aristocrats of pain.
Now loneliness and depression are my friends
as I lay out silver halide salts, acetic acids,
dishes, trays and tanks of fixer, then climb
into the bath fully clothed to watch the red curve
seep across my white wrist, camera at the ready.

Blow by Blow

for Isabella Blow

Your natural habitat was *Tatler*,
your hats the big-game kind: veiled antlers,
a mound of green ostrich feathers

that wouldn't fit through the door,
a jewel-encrusted lobster.
Wallis Simpson as dressed by Salvador Dali.

No stranger to scandal
your grandfather sold the family estates
to pay his gambling debts,

and was tried in Kenya for the murder
of the lover of his second wife.
Your explorer granny 'dined' in the jungle

on human flesh. Ten years after
that hot morning – your mother retouching
her lipstick in the upstairs glass, your

little brother drowning in the garden pond –
she shook you by the hand, then left.
You were just fourteen.

For dinner that first night you wore
a silver skirt, your little feet shod in
Manolo Blahniks, your mouth a slash of red,

and though we fucked like rabbits
we were two exotic fruits that never bred.
Then it was horse tranquilisers, before

throwing yourself over Hammersmith flyover,
smashing both your legs.
Condemned to flat shoes

you missed that season's collections:
didn't consider Clarks or electro-therapy
a winning cat-walk look. Ovarian cancer

next, then paraquat sipped like martini
from a fluted cocktail glass.
At Gloucester Cathedral a sea of white roses

and six plumed black horses.
Celebrities, paparazzi,
and nothing left, except the crumpled air.

Black Widow

The birds are singing in the trees
and it will soon be over. I thought
of you today, imagining how you'd
feel. I was so happy to be of help,
laying out your clean white shirt,
the ironed linen blessed with my
prayers, loading the belt for the
journey to Checkpoint 5. I was
prepared for your death but not
your failure. The premature explosion
that stole your martyrdom
was just too much to bear. I could
survive your shattered body
but not the shame.
All week, I shut myself in my room,
ate bread and salt, would not answer
till they broke down the door.
At first they laughed: a woman!
Then grasped the sense. Outside I could
hear them throwing stones.
In my *wasiyyah*, I left my face uncovered,
my dark hair lose about my shoulders,
learnt the speech by heart, talking straight
to the camera speaking of your talent
for electronics, the way you fixed
the neighbour's fridge, their flickering TV.
This morning I bathed with special care,
binding the belt beneath my *hijab*.

Now, as I climb from the car to walk
towards the wall, I understand where
submission to God begins. A minute
later the flash, a muffled boom, then a column
of smoke as the driver pulls away
in a trail of dust and I hear him laugh:
'God is great, the stupid woman did it.'
But as the blackness descends,
I know you're waiting for me,
there, among the cool gardens.

III

The Idea of
Islands

Dreaming of Islands

There are two kinds of islands:
those born of erasure and fracture,
cut off from their rocky
birth mothers that drift away
towards some half-imagined
dream, some picture of home –
not a creation, but a re-creation,
not a birth, but a re-birth;
while those created from
the accretions of rosy coral,
or from underwater eruptions,
that bring to light movement
from the lowest depths
dark as our hidden fears,
suggest the earth
lurks like some great beast
beneath the waves
gathering its muscular
strength to punch through
the world's watery skin.
Some islands rise slowly,
others disappear only
to return ghostly as memories
we thought we'd lost:
a landscape of shadowed voices,
beating wings and tumbling streams
where we're not so estranged
from the language of stars.
To live on an island is a form
of forgetting – a drift towards

a brave new world.
Remember the ark set down
on that sole dry ridge,
a place made sacred
by the massive expanse
of the flood? So an island is
what the ocean surrounds:
the deserted reflected back
to itself in a mirroring sea.

Ballinskelligs

They come to me in dreams
Scariff and Deenish, rising like those islands
floating in a veil of mist in Japanese prints,

their peaks in a halo of cloud.
Early morning the sun casts
rings of bright water, stepping stones of light

out to the distant shore. Midnight
and the islands are sleeping, turned in
on their own emptiness as if remembering

those ghostly lives gleaned on the barren cliffs
stinking of sea birds and herring,
the air thick with turf and old rain.

Now they've gone, they lie empty as picked
crab shells, the battering sea splattering
their glassy rocks with the spittle of lost tongues.

Outside my window the strait is moon-streaked,
silver as a hairline crack across
an old mirror. It's as if I could simply rise

from this bed and walk to that distant shore.
Yet the night holds its secrets.
To feel this flat blackness, where even

the stars are hidden, is to understand what
we cannot see at the edge of this visible world.

The single blip of the lighthouse appears,

then disappears every fifteen seconds,
its pulsing beam tracing an arc
across the endless sky, a blinking Cyclops

in the inky dark, till suddenly its morning
and the sun comes up;
streaks of blood-red leaching into the grey.

Cill Rialaig

A drunken wind blew all night,
banging at doors, rattling windows
ill fitting as old men's teeth.

Now that it's day,
I understand the loneliness
of storms as the distant island

beckons in the mist
like a half-remembered dream.
This is the edge of the world;

these wrecked cottages
have lost their hearts,
now they stare out to sea

granite-faced as grieving widows.
Their very stones breathe
destitution and loss.

Only the sodden sheep
chewing its cud
by the barbed wire fence

seems at home
in these blighted fields.
How many loved, lost,

then left these peat-blackened hearths,
these gorse hedgerows,
backs hunched

against bone-chilling spray,
the print of hunger branded
on their lips?

In the high fields
standing stones lean against
the battering wind like ghosts,

like keening women,
the gusts unravelling them,
grief hanging in the air like rain.

The Idea of Islands

The candle in its glass stutters,
   reflected back fourfold
      in the panes of this small window,

though tonight there is no moon,
   only an endless sea black
      as spilt ink

and waves crested with white horses
   stretching into the far distance like light
      streaking the surface of a dark negative.

I know that out there
   there is not nothing;
      for my mind recalls the idea of islands

and how in the early morning mist
   high above the boiling sea
      mercury clouds

can part
   suddenly as quicksilver
      to reveal a radiant light.

Though I have been here before
   I now understand something of
      the compulsion of departure and return,

how love must be a surrender,
   a letting go of that dark grieving
      lodged in marrow bone,

and how life is only this moment
   at midnight: a guttering candle
      and a terrible wind

howling across a strait of wide water,
   like something lost in the anthracite dark
      beating its way home in the battering rain.

Going Back

What figures are these
coming across the high fields
through a shroud of mist

above Baile 'n Sgeilg
smelling of turfsmoke and herring,
their veins webbed maps

of stone and straw, their hearts
heavy with the weight of digging,
here where they knew no plough

and traces of potato ridges still poke
from the wasted earth between
the broken vertebrae of boundary walls?

I think of the woman I thought
I saw bent beneath
bronchitis and rain

and wonder why I came back;
what it is we search for in
return and remembering?

My tiny window opens onto sea
and starlight, blueblacks
and charcoal greys, as I give myself up

to the salty bellowing, the low voices
muttering in the healing dark;
to the hallucination of what remains.

Migrations

Late winter afternoon;
the light shrunk to long shadows
hunched beneath the barn

and a scribble of crows
wheeling in the tractor's wake
above the furrowed fields.

There is such loneliness
among these ragged wings
where something is stirring in the blood,

a gathering disquiet, as the raucous
cries stain the wind black as ink.
December dusk

and the grey sky lies in tatters
along the hedgerows.
Some deep imperative

compels this tribal gathering,
this restless leaving;
the tilting of a hundred tiny

hearts, each pointing
like the needles of a compass
towards a dream of home.

New Year

Whited-out morning,
every movement erased
in this silvery vacancy,

nothing has form,
all is shift and flux
and the motions of mind

have nothing
to hang onto
here in this milky mist

where the only black
thing is a crow pecking
at bleached bones

half buried in mud.
Will the next hour look
like this, tomorrow

like today or will I wake
and from my small
window see the shimmering

cadences of ocean,
its tentative tracery of gold
written on the waves

like prayers and the islands
rising with new meaning
in the January dawn?

St. Fionán

Soaked in ash and sea water,
the yellow fat

scraped off with knives,
we dressed

the tanned leather
with sheep tallow,

polished it smooth
with stones before stretching

the stinking hide
over the arched ribs

of the wooden *curach*
lashing with thongs,

till our fingers bled,
the three chiselled benches

for the oarsmen to sit in pairs:
those chosen to bear us

to the place
of our resurrection.

Night,
and we drift beneath

a rosary of stars,
bony faces bowed in

the cathedral dark,
as our oars pull against

the freezing surf.
Days we have waited

for fair weather,
now faith and the foul flesh

of salted sea birds
must sustain us as we

set sail towards the edge
of the world,

following one another
into this penitent dark.

Odyssey

A metallic sky fills
with the screech and stench
of seabirds,

and the ordure of guano
clings to the wind as
the horizon tilts

and the skelligs rise
like something dreamt,
Wagnerian in the silvery fog.

Solitude,
prayer, atonement?
What desire for holiness

brought them, now brings us here,
pilgrims
in this watery wilderness

where what we've left behind
and what we will become
remains hidden in this muslin mist.

Terns loop above the waves
inscribing scriptures
in the rain soaked air.

My heart stilled,
speechless,
listens for sermons

on the wind's breath,
knowing that life's
not

what was expected;
understanding
how old I have become.

Jimmy Murphy

Hunched beneath its corrugated cowl high
on Bólus Head, smoke curls from the squat stack
    of the lime-washed cottage, its storm-proof windows
tiny as green fish eyes, turned from the lashed Atlantic.

All night it has rained, water sluicing down
the muddy track between sea-worn pebbles
    that decorate the path from his careful peat stack
to the freshly-painted door.

Beyond the sheep-chewed turf and dry stone wall
islands float on the bay's mirror
    fragile as promises in the January mist.
Pyjamas snap in the savage wind.

This morning he is out among the clouds,
high on the mountain tending his flock,
    their woolly backsides smeared in Day-Glo pink
like muddy go-go dancers shimmying up the tussocked hills.

It is in his bones this loneliness;
the deep winter dark where a half-forgotten kiss
    returns like something once dreamt.
Now his days are a catechism of liniments

and sheep dip. Nights the dying turf glints
rose-patterned china, the photo of his mother, as
    he throws a final clod upon the hearth.
He is the last; these patchwork fields,

the ocean's relentless pull
all root him to this wasted, brutal land,
    as each night he climbs the tiny staircase
to his narrow bed beneath a halo of freezing stars.

Bólus Head

Early morning and the islands
barely visible in the mist.
Across the strait,

wide as the distance between this
waking and my dreams,
wave enfolds wave

like a series of thoughts,
as the wind snatches droplets
from the ocean's cold surface to scatter

over the raddled ridges
in a shower of April rain.
Here water endlessly adapts,

fluid against the rigidity of rock,
to seep through gilded gorse
and rocky outcrop to become

a spring, a stream, a river
before returning to its home,
the sea.

Though we feel ourselves
to be made from earth,
our cells are filled with water.

See this grass,
these tufted patches of silver
and brown shivering behind

the dry stone wall,
and the solitary violet
hunkered against the wind,

what do they tell us?
That this wasted land
is the heart's last outpost;

and when on rain swept afternoons
we hold our breath,
hoping for fragile fingers

of sunlight to break
through the louring clouds,
that although such iridescence

does not erase
this vast emptiness,
for a moment –

as the rays crest the pewter water –
we are not so alone
in this disappearing world.

Five Ways of Looking at Islands

mid-distance:
    the islands purple against
        a widow-weed sea
foreground:
    spittle-white surf
      running-running
        below jigsaw cliffs
close-up:
    a tussock of reeds (ochre, umber?)
      vibrates in the high wind
      and a shredded sliver of (blue) fertilizer bag
        flaps
      on the barbed wire fence –
as the black dot of crow
      pecks
    the bleached skull of a dead sheep –
my fingers freezing

1.05

a slant of light breaks
                    through plum coloured clouds,
            though there are no doves
                    and no chorus of angels,
just the hump-backed islands
        lit now with a greater clarity
                    and a solitary gannet,
with nothing to think about,
                    gliding the swell

1.10

the unravelling wind
        icy in the tunnel of my ear –

            such stillness
as the land's curved hip nestles
        for shelter
                in the granite hollow

1.17

my heart
            opening to all this;
                        wind, rain, surf,
the shifting nature of things

1.20

        in the distance
the islands veiled in a dull patina of mist,
knowing, now, that I will never go there . . .

then a soft inhalation,
a letting go . . .
                    of all the words for love . . .

Bronchitis

For days before Christmas
a chronic infection of the lungs,
bacteria pooling in the damp folds

of the bronchioles, and the damaged cilla
unable to push up the glutinous green
mucus into the cold bathroom sink

so it gathers like diesel sludge
in the fevered recesses.
Now as the year turns

I wake in this little cottage
wheezing to the sound of rain
as across the bay,

and fog-bound centuries
I hear them out there
on the mist-bound Skellig,

chests full of faith and phlegm,
chilblained fingers bloodied
by salt wind, their sandaled feet

slapping over the wet stones
towards the Matins bell.
To live is an act of faith,

each day returning
with its small cruelties relentless
as the incoming tide.

Here on the edge
of the whip-lashed Atlantic,
the snarls and knots of the body

chart what only the body can understand
as the broken hinges of the heart
lie splayed, bruised by endless rain.

Small Hours

And who would even hear if I called out in this black night?
The cold stars in the cloud strewn sky above the sleeping
islands that shine indifferent as stars, that are not even looked
at? For what vast emptiness is out there as I huddle beneath two
duvets, my feet freezing in this small bed under the windy
eaves, here, on the edge of the Atlantic, rocked by an immense swell?
Can skin that is untouched remain alive to the possibilities of
another dawn after these fragile hours, restless on the rim of
the world? It is too far out to where the seductive beam of the
lighthouse beckons like a callous lover; for between us are cold
cold miles and the way barely visible in the dense dark.

Possibility

But what sort of faded word is radiant to describe this early
spring sun burnishing the far waves as a piano concerto spills from
the battered mahogany radio, out through the fresh-flung door
into the stony sun-flecked fields? How are we to speak of such
transience in this obdurate world? A solitary gull wheels over
the granite rocks buffeted by a bridal swell, a blade of grass
shivers, held by a single stone. Cicatrices of gorse flash on the
hill's flank above the tin coloured sea and I feel a surge of grief
at the impossibility of connection. For it is too late to talk of
beauty, to talk of love, though I have more loving within than
those who are easily loved. Standing in this white gleam of
morning the sun pours through the roof of my mouth, filling
the fields, the sky, the clouds, as I struggle to feel the shape
of possibility growing inside me – the green fuse, the quiet
heart beating – as moss, ferns, and foxgloves, cowered by this
relentless wind, stir in the frozen ground.

Uíbh Ráthach

Why return? Because it's like this: the heart-wrench
  of eel-call from the Sargasso deep, a liminal notion of
origins and home. Not in the sense of threshold or hearth
  but something closer to that elusive knowledge of self
we experience by the sea. Close your eyes. What do you feel
  when those briny gusts whip through the grass along
the strand and the wind off the sea chases round the ruined priory,
  winkling its weathered headstones, its plaster Madonna
in her goldfish dome of glass, the silken flowers sodden
  and tattered by rain? Is this why you come back?
For this sense of fixity, for the comfort of their belief?
  To write your signature with driftwood in wet sand,
  for all that is unchanging; resistant even to the seduction
  of moonlight brushing the sea's wrinkled surface
like a gigolo caressing tired skin?
  Listen to this rain-washed silence. No, not exactly silence –
for there's always the trickle of freshwater streams unfurling
  across the wet sand, that pull of surf crunching
like a neighbour's car on midnight gravel,
  or the wind mewing between loose cottage tiles insistent
as a shut-out cat – some essence behind the primary hush:
  a pulse, a throb deep in the aorta of things.
Stand still. Wait. How fragile it all is. The tide receding
  and returning until nothing can be separated out:
everything merging on the wind's out-breath in a single name.

...*yes*

The wind writes untranslatable hieroglyphs on the sea's surface
  as the tide recedes leaving a ragged hemline
stitched with shells along the rim of wet sand before returning
  again and again, though never quite the same, and always indifferent.

Feathers, driftwood, wave-smoothed fragments of glass,
  what is there to believe in except this mineral world
as I stand on an empty Irish beach stripped to the bone
  by freezing squalls? Before I left the city I woke to a bird

singing its heart out at midnight in the tree beside my window
  as if it was dawn. What sense can be made of things
when all that's left of a young man stabbed beneath
  a ribbon of Christmas lights is a clutch of garage flowers?

I had hoped for miracles; from this El Greco light breaking
  through the purple clouds over the islands, to the taste of sex on the
    tongue –
the merging of I with you to form something radiant - but instead found
  only the monastic chill of daybreak where even angels refuse to sing.

With the tide's turn scum gathers at the sea's edge; kelp, a plastic shoe,
  bob on the current as the morning slips through my fingers like sand,
like love, and the tireless waves push on into their own future, as I reach
  for a pen, struggling to transcribe word by word, sentence by sentence,
    this fragile

                                                              ...*yes*

Notes

THE FORGETTING AND REMEMBERING OF AIR: I am indebted
for the title to a chapter in *The Spell of the Sensuous: Perception and
Language in a More-Than-Human World*. David Abram. Vintage
Books. New York. 1996.

THE ICE SHIP: In 1762 the English trading ship Octavius hazarded
the uncharted Northwest Passage back from a successful trip to the
orient and became trapped in pack-ice. In 1775 it was discovered
by the whaler Herald adrift near Greenland, the bodies of its crew
frozen on deck.

KLEIN'S BLUE: Yves Klein's photograph 'Leap into the Void' shows
him floating over a street in an apparent bid to overcome gravity.
A believer in Rosicrucianism, his pigment, Kleinian Blue, became
known as IKB.

THE FALL: Margaret Moyes' was one of the few suicides to achieve
a notoriety akin to that of Victorian murder cases. The press
enthusiastically took on the job of interpreting the event for those
not present.

DORA: The painter Dora Carrington committed suicide two months
after the death of her homosexual lover, the writer Lytton Strachey,
shooting herself with a gun borrowed from her friend, Hon. Bryan
Guinness. In 1921 she'd married Ralph Partridge. Carrington,
Partridge, and Strachey had shared a Wiltshire farm-house, Ham
Spray.

EVA: Hitler's dog was called Blondi.

EVE ARNOLD REMEMBERS: The photographer Eve Arnold
photographed Marilyn Monroe on many occasions and developed
an especially close relationship with her over a number of years.

[87]

NOTE TO TED: Assia Wevill, Ted Hughes' mistress during his marriage to Sylvia Plath, gassed herself in copy cat manner to Plath taking her and Hughes' daughter, Shura, with her.

LAST SUPPER: The photographer Diane Arbus was found fully clothed in the bath, her wrists slit and a note that said 'Last Supper.' There are rumours that she photographed her own death. But no such photos were found.

BLOW BY BLOW: the eldest child of Major Sir Evelyn Delves Broughton, Isabella Blow, was a magazine editor, international style icon and the muse of hat designer Philip Treacy.

BLACK WIDOW: relies on an account about female suicide bombers found on the internet. *Wasiyyah*: Islamic last will and testament.

DREAMING OF ISLANDS: was inspired by the essay Desert Islands from *Desert Islands and Other Texts 1953–1974* Gilles Deleuze.

ST. FIONÁN: was a follower of St Brendan, and is attributed with founding the monastery on Skellig Michael.